Bootstrap
Reference Guide

Published on February 1, 2019

This is a great book. It puts a lot of very **helpful resources at your fingertips** *that would take a great deal of time to pull together on your own.*

— *susannetic, Amazon Review*

*It's just as advertised, **listings of Bootstrap syntax that can be a handy reference when building an application.** You could build the lists yourself from the internet, but why, when this handy reference does it.*

— David Kirk, Amazon Review

*I appreciate the **concise** style of the Bootstrap reference book,*

— Charles R.

Table of Contents

Dedicated to my boys Marcus and Joshua, may you learn to discover, develop, and share your God-given talents.
Matthew 25:14-30

Jacob Lett is the author of the *Bootstrap 4 Quick Start*, and the *Bootstrap Reference Guide*. He strives to help web developers save time learning how to design and build responsive websites.
www.linkedin.com/in/jacoblett/

Bootstrap Reference Guide

Jacob Lett
Copyright © 2019 by Jacob Lett

Publisher

Bootstrap Creative
Sterling Heights, Michigan 48314
(586) 894-8024
Find us on the web at: bootstrapcreative.com

To report errors, please send an email to support@bootstrapcreative.com

Notice of Rights

Notice of Liability

Trademarks

ISBN: 978-1-7322058-3-3

Introduction

Building websites today is a lot more challenging and time consuming than it used to be.

Some of my first websites were first designed in Adobe Photoshop,® exported to HTML tables (yes tables) and then linked together with Adobe Dreamweaver.® If your website did not exceed the width of common monitor resolutions (1024px by 768px) everything would work out fine.

Web standards[1] were quickly introduced because using table markup for grid layout is just bad practice. So HTML tables were replaced with floated divs and tag markup that had meaning – referred to as semantics. This also shifted things away from the majority of the visual design being baked into images and now relying on CSS3 to create borders, shadows, rounded corners, etc.

The first widely used CSS grid system was the 960 grid system (Fig. 1) created by Nathan Smith. This 12,16, 24 column grid system was designed to work well for a fixed desktop resolution of 1024px x 768px. This grid system was widely used and helped designers and developers work from the same grid pixel dimensions.

Fig. 1: The 960 grid system helped bring consistency between grid design in Photoshop and the web.

Then in 2007, Steve Jobs introduced the world to the iPhone with Multi-Touch gestures[2]. Now people could access websites anywhere using just their fingers.

Web designers and developers had to quickly develop creative solutions to work within the new constraints presented by smartphones and tablets.

---

1   https://www.goodreads.com/book/show/259072.Designing_With_Web_Standards
2   http://www.lukew.com/ff/entry.asp?1071

 BootstrapCreative

These Constraints Include:

- Smaller screens
- Increased pixel densities with retina displays
- Ability to switch between portrait and landscape orientation
- Multi-touch gestures
- Slower data connections
- Distracted user attention (one eyeball and one thumb).

At the start, the concept of responsive design did not exist. And so mobile devices had to scale down websites to fit the smaller screens. For the user, in order to read the text they would have to double tap the screen or pinch and zoom.

Website owners quickly realized it was not a good experience to display their homepage at a zoomed in level. The meta tag below was introduced to remove this default scaling and give the site creator more control. When this meta tag is added to the <head> of a page, it instructs the web browser to scale the document 100% to prevent pinch/zoom on mobile.

```
<meta name="viewport" content="width=device-width, initial-scale=1">
```

Different Mobile Strategies

Mobile Applications

One approach is to build a dedicated experience as a mobile app. This gives the developer the most control and could utilize the device user interface components and to help with navigation. Major drawbacks include: it requires an app developer, considerable amount of marketing to direct existing traffic to download the mobile app, and overcoming low rates of user adoption. Also, any links to outside pages required them to open in a web browser window.

Adaptive Design

Another approach is to build multiple versions of a website and use server side detection to then present custom code for that device or viewport size.

You could decide to have your mobile site on a separate domain for example m.domain.com. The server will then automatically serve all mobile traffic to that domain. The server could also perform dynamic serving of page content so that you have just one domain name. The downsides to this approach is it requires complex server side detection code and is harder to maintain multiple site versions.

Responsive Design

Responsive design was introduced to help designers build one site on one domain that responds to a users viewport. The two necessary elements for a responsive design are a meta viewport tag to disable scaling and media queries to alter the design as the page gets smaller. Responsive design is a lot less expensive and easier to maintain than the other mobile strategies. This has added to its rapid growth and adoption.

A big challenge with responsive design is finding a balance between the content needs for both mobile and desktop. A desktop site has a lot of visual real estate that is often filled with carousels, videos, large parallax background images, and large blocks of text.

If you load a feature-rich website on a mobile device you often increase the page load for mobile visitors. This is due to the large images and videos which are scaled down to mobile.

End-users don't care about your responsive web or your separate sites, **they just want to be able to get stuff done quickly.**

—— Brad Frost, author of Atomic Design

Mobile First

In the desktop first approach, you sacrifice the mobile experience because you have a lot of images and text content. In an article from Zurb on mobile first design it said, "Roughly 80% of the screen size is taken away when you start with mobile first design, you have to think about how to utilize your space in a much more conservative manner."

 BootstrapCreative

Fig. 2 - Desktop First Responsive Site

	Desktop	Mobile
Data Speed	Fast	Slow
Width	Wide	Narrow
Height	Unlimited	Unlimited
Retina Display Probability	Medium	High
Page File Size	Large	Large

A mobile first approach considers the goals of a mobile user and presents the content to help them achieve those goals. It removes all of the fluff and filler content and presents a concise collection of content that loads fast and is easy to use.

Fig 3. Mobile First Responsive Site

	Mobile	Desktop
Data Speed	Slow	Fast
Width	Narrow	Wide
Height	Unlimited	Unlimited
Retina Display Probability	High	Medium
Page File Size	Small	Medium +

The chart above shows the workflow flipped so the site is built mobile first and then enhancements are added as the viewport gets wider. Notice how the mobile site is loading a small file size on a slow data speed? That is as Google would say, being mobile friendly. But some might say. "Ok now the mobile site looks good but now the desktop looks too basic and lacks flair."

Progressive Enhancement

A great way to solve this is to progressively enhance the page as your data speed and screen width increases. Everything you add to the page will be enhancing the design and if it doesn't load for some reason your page is still usable.

Screens are small, connections are slow, and people often only give you their partial attention or short bursts of their time. **Designing for mobile first forces you to embrace these constraints**

—— Luke Wroblewski, Mobile First

The best way to do this is with JavaScript media queries[3] to determine viewport width and then load in content to the page. I created a small plugin called IfBreakpoint.js[4] to help detect Bootstrap 4 breakpoints with JavaScript. I also recommend reading this article[5] on ways to progressively load images with media queries.

One creative solution that has transformed the web and made responsive design easier for web designers has been the Bootstrap frontend framework. We will take a closer look at Bootstrap in the next section.

---

3   https://jacoblett.github.io/IfBreakpoint/
4   https://jacoblett.github.io/IfBreakpoint/
5   https://timkadlec.com/2012/04/media-query-asset-downloading-results/

What is Bootstrap?

I remember building my first few responsive websites. I wasted so much time writing the same type of styles over and over for each new project. I also found it difficult to find plugins that worked well together and had cohesive design style

I then heard about Bootstrap and I liked how it included javascript components and had really comprehensive documentation. The documentation was extremely detailed and easy to follow. At first, it was hard to know what classes did what but after using it on a few projects I was amazed at how quickly I could create a working prototype of a design. The time I saved enabled me to complete more projects in less time and make more money in the process.

The more I used Bootstrap, the more I felt like it could be a global standard because it removes a lot of routine tasks when building responsive sites.

Bootstrap was created by Mark Otto and Jacob Thornton[6] at Twitter as a framework to encourage consistency across internal tools. It is now an open source project hosted on GitHub[7] and has seen rapid growth and global use in web applications and websites.

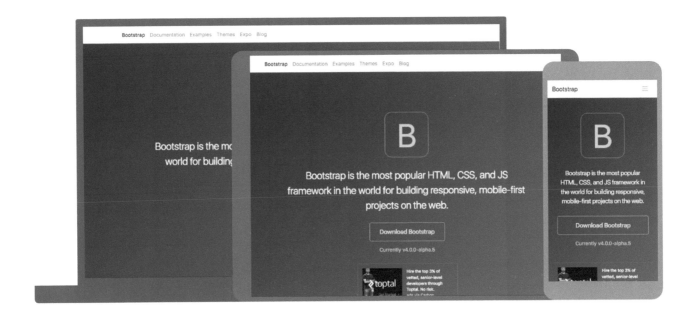

---

6   https://v4-alpha.getbootstrap.com/about/history/

7   https://github.com/twbs/bootstrap

Bootstrap CSS Framework History

- Before 2011   An internal Twitter tool
- August 2011   Released as open source
- January 2012   Bootstrap 2
- August 2013   Bootstrap 3
- August 2015   Bootstrap 4 Alpha
- August 2017   Bootstrap 4 Beta
- January 2018   Bootstrap 4

A Toolkit Built in Style Guide Form

When Bootstrap was first created at Twitter it was built as a toolkit of reusable components with additional documentation and code snippets on how to use them. This helped a team of multiple developers work on a project and have a cohesive methodology on how to build layouts. The documentation and ease of implementation, made it easy to share and reference with others, regardless of their skill level.

So, **the initial intent of Bootstrap was to be a living style guide documentation for a team of developers** to code in the same way following a set of pre-defined rules and components.

Today, Bootstrap Can Be Used in Two Main Ways:

Linking to a precompiled version via CDN or locally

Linking to a customized build using the Sass source files

On the next page (Fig. 5) I explore the pros and cons of each method and also break them into smaller sub-methods to help you decide which is best for your project.

BootstrapCreative

A System of Components

At this point, you might be wondering what is a component and why does Bootstrap use them? Well, one definition I found was, "A component is a minimal software item that can be tested in isolation." The keyword in that phrase is **isolation**.

Since CSS cascades down to child elements, how do you isolate things and write styles to target specific components and leave everything as is? The solution Bootstrap presented is the use of prefix class naming and sub-classes for variations.

Mark Otto wrote on his blog[1], "Each class name begins with a prefix. Class name prefixing makes our code more durable and easier to maintain, but it also better enables us to **scope styles to only the relevant elements.**"

Is Bootstrap Even Necessary?

If you are an experienced web designer or developer you are probably wondering what the benefits are using Bootstrap in your project. Prior to using Bootstrap, I used a boilerplate I wrote myself that consisted of a reset, basic grid, typography, utilities, and media queries. Below are the benefits I have experienced from now using Bootstrap for my projects.

Helps You Save Time

I admit I was the worst at documenting my own work. I would use my boilerplate on a project and then want to make an update to it a month later. But by then, I totally forgot my naming convention. So I would have to spend time reading my code to try to understand what I did. If I couldn't figure it out, I would add new code and leave the old code alone to prevent breaking something. Yup, sound the code bloat alarm.

Bootstrap has amazing documentation on each component. So if I want to update a project I worked on a few months ago that uses Bootstrap I know where to go to find documentation if I get stuck. Also, the more I use Bootstrap the more it is burned into my brain and the less time is spent searching the documentation.

---

1   http://markdotto.com/2012/03/02/stop-the-cascade/

Helps You Avoid Cross-browser Bugs

Prior to using Bootstrap I would get the dreaded emails from clients saying their website they just paid me for doesn't look good on X device. And of course, it is a device I do not currently own or have access to. After hours or searching on Google you finally find a fix on Stack Overflow. You find comfort knowing it is a common problem with Android devices and not something you caused.

Being an open source project, anyone can submit browser bugs and code fixes for it. This is an extremely valuable asset to a developer because you gain confidence knowing your code has been improved by a community to address common browser bugs. No matter how good you are, there is no way you can be aware of every browser inconsistency and the fix necessary. Using Bootstrap, you're standing on the shoulders of giants.

Helps You Follow Best Practices

I studied graphic design in college and self-taught myself HTML & CSS from books, YouTube, and blog posts. This mixture of knowledge worked to some degree but I know there are a lot of knowledge gaps. I hit my lack of understanding head-on when I first learned Bootstrap with all of the new terminology written for software engineers.

Bootstrap is not just a framework but a methodology of best practices for front-end design.

Gather a room full of the smartest web designers and developers and let them discuss at length what they think is the best way to write CSS and to organize a project. The result being a distilled version of best practices agreed upon by a large collection of your peers.

Helps You Avoid jQuery Plugin Soup

I know some JavaScript but writing a full-fledged plugin is out of my reach. So I often collected various jQuery plugins into a project to achieve the look and functionality I was looking for.

But I often ran into the following problems:

- Plugins would not work across browsers
- Plugin CSS styles would conflict with other CSS styles
- Plugins would be dependent on different versions of jQuery

Bootstrap contains a collection of jQuery components that you know are stable on modern browsers compatible and works with your jQuery version. Also, the styling matches all of the other components in the your project.

Helps You Be More Marketable

Bootstrap has 73% of the design framework market share[2] as of May 2017. This popularity correlates to the demand for people to know the framework to either update existing systems and or create new ones.

So this will make you more marketable to prospective employers. Indeed.com, a popular job search engine, shows Bootstrap has a lot of job postings compared to other CSS frameworks.

Framework Name	Total Sites
Bootstrap CSS (update to v4?)	12,559,226
HTML5 Boilerplate	4,219,959
960 Grid System	437,120
Unsemantic	74,386
Semantic UI	10,803

Source: BuiltWith as of May, 2017[3]

---

2   https://trends.builtwith.com/docinfo/design-framework

3   https://trends.builtwith.com/docinfo/design-framework

How to Install Bootstrap

All you need to do is add the Bootstrap CSS to the HEAD of your page and the javascript to the page. In order to use the JavaScript behavior you also need to have jQuery and popper.js loaded before bootstrap.js.

Here is an example

```
<!DOCTYPE html>
<html lang="en">
  <head>
    <!-- Required meta tags -->
    <meta charset="utf-8">
    <meta name="viewport" content="width=device-width, initial-scale=1, shrink-to-fit=no">
    <!-- Bootstrap CSS -->
    <link rel="stylesheet" href="https://stackpath.bootstrapcdn.com/bootstrap/4.2.1/css/bootstrap.min.css">
    <!-- Your CSS -->
    <link rel="stylesheet" href="css/main.css">
  </head>
  <body>
    <div class="container">
      <h1>Hello, world!</h1>
    </div>
    <!-- jQuery first, then Tether, then Bootstrap JS. -->
    <script src="https://code.jquery.com/jquery-3.3.1.slim.min.js"></script>
<script src="https://cdnjs.cloudflare.com/ajax/libs/popper.js/1.14.6/umd/popper.min.js"></script>
<script src="https://stackpath.bootstrapcdn.com/bootstrap/4.2.1/js/bootstrap.min.js"></script>
    <!-- Your JS -->
    <script src="js/main.js"></script>
  </body>
</html>
```

Summary

When your time is billable, every minute you shave off will greatly improve your bottom line. Plus it makes development more fun because you are not declaring redundant CSS properties.

I hope I have shown you how Bootstrap can save you time and make you a better developer in the process. In addition, you will be following industry best practices vetted by an open source community.

Now that you know the history and benefits of using Bootstrap let's dive into what's new in version 4.

Responsive Design Introduction Video

Want to learn more about responsive web design and the mobile-first workflow?

Watch a 45 minute training video at https://bootstrapcreative.com/b4recording

Introduction

Bootstrap 4

Bootstrap 4.2.1

CSS

```
<link rel="stylesheet" href="https://stackpath.bootstrapcdn.com/bootstrap/4.2.1/css/
bootstrap.min.css" integrity="sha384-GJzZqFGwb1QTTN6wy59ffF1BuGJpLSa9DkKMp0DgiMDm4iYMj
70gZWKYbI706tWS" crossorigin="anonymous">
```

JS

JS is only necessary if you plan on using one or all of the following components: Alerts, Buttons, Carousel, Collapse, Dropdowns, Modals, Navbar, Tooltips and Scrollspy

```
<script src="https://code.jquery.com/jquery-3.3.1.slim.min.js" integrity="sha384-q8i/X+
965Dz00rT7abK41JStQIAqVgRVzpbzo5smXKp4YfRvH+8abtTE1Pi6jizo" crossorigin="anonymous"></
script>
```

```
<script src="https://cdnjs.cloudflare.com/ajax/libs/popper.js/1.14.6/umd/popper.min.
js" integrity="sha384-wHAiFfRlMFy6i5SRaxvfOCifBUQy1xHdJ/yoi7FRNXMRBu5WHdZYu1hA6ZOblgut"
crossorigin="anonymous"></script>
```

```
<script src="https://stackpath.bootstrapcdn.com/bootstrap/4.2.1/js/bootstrap.min.js"
integrity="sha384-B0UglyR+jN6CkvvICOB2joaf5I4l3gm9GU6Hc1og6Ls7i6U/mkkaduKaBhlAXv9k"
crossorigin="anonymous"></script>
```

Components

Alerts	List group
Badge	Media Object
Breadcrumb	Modal
Buttons	Navs
Button group	Navbar
Card	Pagination
Carousel	Popovers
Collapse	Progress
Dropdowns	Scrollspy
Forms	Spinners
Input group	Toasts
Jumbotron	Tooltips

Utilities

Borders	Sizing
Clearfix	Spacing
Close icon	Text
Colors	Vertical align
Display	Visibility
Embed	
Flex	
Float	
Image replacement	
Position	
Screenreaders	
Shadows	

BootstrapCreative

Breakpoints

Extra small devices (portrait phones, less than 576px) do not require a breakpoint because Bootstrap 4 is mobile first.

Breakpoints | Max container width

not needed=Extra small < 576px | None (auto)

sm=Small ≥ 576px | 540px

md=Medium ≥ 768px | 720px

lg=Large ≥ 992px | 960px

xl=Extra large ≥ 1200px | 1140px

Media Queries

Change the width value to set a media query for sm, md, lg, xl.

```
/* Small devices (landscape phones, 576px and up) */
@media (min-width: 576px) { }
```

Lists

.list-unstyled Removes default list margin

.dl-horizontal Makes list items two columns

.list-inline Makes list items inline

.list-inline-item Added to each li

Example

```
<ul class="social-icons list-inline">
<li class="list-inline-item">item 1</li>
</ul>
```

Typography

.text-left Left aligned text

.text-*-left Left aligned by breakpoint

.text-center Center aligned text

.text-right Right aligned text

.text-justify Justified text

.text-nowrap No wrap text

.text-(lowercause, uppercase, capitalize) Changes the text capitalization style

.text-decoration-none Removes decoration

.text-truncate Truncate text with ellipsis

.lead Good for first paragraph of article

.text-monospace Changes to monospace font

.font-weight-(bold, bolder, normal, light, lighter, italic) Changes the font weight

.blockquote Slightly increases font-size and sets a bottom margin for blockquotes

.(h1, h2, h3, h4, h5, h6) Used to make an element match the heading styles

.display-(1, 2, 3, 4) Large display text. 1=96px, 2=88px, 3=72px, 4=56px

Colors

.text-primary	.bg-primary
.text-secondary	.bg-secondary
.text-success	.bg-success
.text-danger	.bg-danger
.text-warning	.bg-warning
.text-info	.bg-info
.text-light	.bg-light
.text-dark	.bg-dark
.text-body	.bg-white
.text-muted	.bg-transparent
.text-white	
.text-black-50	
.text-white-50	

Images

.img-fluid Make an image responsive

.rounded Adds rounded corners to image

.rounded-circle Crops image to be circle

.img-thumbnail Adds rounded corner and img border

Floats

.float-left Floats item left

.float-right Floats item right

.float-none Removes float

.float-*-* Add breakpoints if needed

Borders

Add border
.border Add border to all sides

.border-* (top, right, bottom, left) Add border on a certain edge

Remove Border
.border-0 Remove border to all sides

.border-*-0 (top, right, bottom, left) Remove border on a certain edge

Border Radius
.rounded Adds border radius on all edges

.rounded-* (top, right, bottom, left, circle) Adds a border radius

.rounded-0 Removes border radius

Display

Value can equal one of the following: none, inline, inline-block, block, table, table-cell, table-row, flex, inline-flex

.d-(value) for xs

.d-(sm, md, lg, and xl)-(value) sets display value for breakpoint and up

Position

.position-(static, relative, absolute, fixed, sticky) Sets CSS position values but not responsive

.fixed-(top, bottom) Position an element to the top of the viewport.

.sticky-top Position an element at the top of the viewport, but only after you scroll past it. Not fully supported in IE.

Shadows

.shadow The regular sized box drop shadow

.shadow-(none, sm, lg) Remove box drop shadow or change its size.

Sizing

Make an element as wide or as tall (relative to its parent)

.w-(5%, 50%, 75%, 100%, auto) Sets width

.h-(5%, 50%, 75%, 100%, auto) Sets height

.mw-(5%, 50%, 75%, 100%, auto) Sets max-width

.mh-(5%, 50%, 75%, 100%, auto) Sets max-height

BootstrapCreative

Spacing

Sides

t= top, b=bottom, l=left, r=right,
x=x axis, y=y-axis

Size

The values for each level of spacing are calculation of the base font size which is 16px or 1rem.

Here the pixel equivalents. 0=0px, 1=4px, 2=2px, 3-16px, 4=24px, 5=48px, auto

.m(t, b, l, r, x, y)-(sm, md, lg, and xl)-(0, 1, 2, 3, 4, 5, auto) Sets margin value, remove breakpoint for xs

.p(t, b, l, r, x, y)-(sm, md, lg, and xl)-(0, 1, 2, 3, 4, 5, auto) Sets padding value, remove breakpoint for xs

.mx-auto Used to horizontally center an element relative to parent container

Negative Margin

Add the letter n in from of the margin size value to apply a negative margin.

For example: .mt-n1 would apply a size 1 negative top margin.

Vertical Align

.align-(baseline, top, middle, bottom, text-top, text-bottom) Changes the vertical alignment of inline, inline-block, inline-table, and table cell elements.

Visibility

These classes do not modify the display property and do not affect layout.

.visible Takes up space and visible
.invisible Takes up space and invisible

Overflow

Set how content overflows a parent element.

.overflow-auto Container will have a scroll if the content overflows
.overflow-hidden The container will not scroll and the content will be cut off.

Screenreaders

.sr-only Only show on screen readers
.sr-only-focusable Show element when it has a focused state

Bootstrap 4

Starter Template

```html
<!DOCTYPE html>
<html lang="en">
  <head>
    <!-- Required meta tags -->
    <meta charset="utf-8">
    <meta name="viewport" content="width=device-width, initial-scale=1, shrink-to-fit=no">
    <!-- Bootstrap CSS -->
    <link rel="stylesheet" href="https://stackpath.bootstrapcdn.com/bootstrap/4.2.1/css/bootstrap.min.css" integrity="sha384-GJzZqFGwb1QTTN6wy59ffF1BuGJpLSa9DkKMp0DgiMDm4iYMj70gZWKYbI706tWS" crossorigin="anonymous">
    <!-- Main CSS -->
    <link rel="stylesheet" href="css/main.css">
  </head>
  <body>
    <div class="container">
      <h1>Hello, world!</h1>
      <div class="row">
          <div class="col-sm-6">Left Column</div>
          <div class="col-sm-6">Right Column</div>
      </div>
    </div>
    <!-- jQuery first, then Tether, then Bootstrap JS. -->
    <script src="https://code.jquery.com/jquery-3.3.1.slim.min.js" integrity="sha384-q8i/X+965Dz00rT7abK41JStQIAqVgRVzpbzo5smXKp4YfRvH+8abtTE1Pi6jizo" crossorigin="anonymous"></script>
    <script src="https://cdnjs.cloudflare.com/ajax/libs/popper.js/1.14.6/umd/popper.min.js" integrity="sha384-wHAiFfRlMFy6i5SRaxvfOCifBUQy1xHdJ/yoi7FRNXMRBu5WHdZYu1hA6ZOblgut" crossorigin="anonymous"></script>
    <script src="https://stackpath.bootstrapcdn.com/bootstrap/4.2.1/js/bootstrap.min.js" integrity="sha384-B0UglyR+jN6CkvvICOB2joaf5I4l3gm9GU6Hc1og6Ls7i6U/mkkaduKaBhlAXv9k" crossorigin="anonymous"></script>
    <!-- Main JS -->
    <script src="js/main.js"></script>
  </body>
</html>
```

One Column Centered Grid

```
<div class="container">
    <div class="row justify-content-
center">
        <div class="col-md-6"></div>
    </div>
</div>
```

Two Column Grid

```
<div class="container">
    <div class="row">
        <div class="col-sm-6"></div>
        <div class="col-sm-6"></div>
    </div>
</div>
```

Three Column Grid

```
<div class="container">
    <div class="row">
        <div class="col-sm-4"></div>
        <div class="col-sm-4"></div>
        <div class="col-sm-4"></div>
    </div>
</div>
```

Four Column Grid

```
<div class="container">
    <div class="row">
        <div class="col-sm-3"></div>
        <div class="col-sm-3"></div>
        <div class="col-sm-3"></div>
        <div class="col-sm-3"></div>
    </div>
</div>
```

Figures

```
<figure class="figure">
    <img src="https://dummyimage.
com/100x100/563d7c/fff&text=+"
class="figure-img img-fluid rounded"
alt="image">
    <figcaption class="figure-caption">A
caption for the above image.</figcaption>
</figure>
```

Media Object

```
<div class="media">
    <img src="https://dummyimage.
com/100x100/563d7c/fff&text=+"
class="mr-3" alt="image">
    <div class="media-body">
        <h5 class="mt-0">Media heading</h5>
        Media object description text
</div>
```

Code

`<code>`

Used to display inline code in a paragraph

`<pre class="pre-scrollable">`

Display multiple lines of code. Use `.pre-scrollable` class to set a max-height of 340px and provide a y-axis scrollbar

`<var>`

Used to display math variables

`<kbd>`

Used to display keyboard input

`<samp>`

Used to display sample output

Navbar

```
<nav class="navbar navbar-toggleable-md navbar-dark bg-primary">
  <button class="navbar-toggler navbar-toggler-right" type="button" data-
toggle="collapse" data-target="#navbarNavDropdown" aria-controls="navbarNavDropdown"
aria-expanded="false" aria-label="Toggle navigation">
    <span class="navbar-toggler-icon"></span>
  </button>
  <a class="navbar-brand" href="#">Navbar</a>
  <div class="collapse navbar-collapse" id="navbarNavDropdown">
    <ul class="navbar-nav">
      <li class="nav-item active">
        <a class="nav-link" href="#">Home <span class="sr-only">(current)</span></a>
      </li>
      <li class="nav-item">
        <a class="nav-link" href="#">Features</a>
      </li>
      <li class="nav-item">
        <a class="nav-link" href="#">Pricing</a>
      </li>
      <li class="nav-item dropdown">
        <a class="nav-link dropdown-toggle" href="http://example.com"
id="navbarDropdownMenuLink" data-toggle="dropdown" aria-haspopup="true" aria-
expanded="false">
          Dropdown link
        </a>
        <div class="dropdown-menu" aria-labelledby="navbarDropdownMenuLink">
          <a class="dropdown-item" href="#">Action</a>
          <a class="dropdown-item" href="#">Another action</a>
          <a class="dropdown-item" href="#">Something else here</a>
        </div>
      </li>
    </ul>
  </div>
</nav>
```

Modal

```html
<!-- Button trigger modal -->
<button type="button" class="btn btn-primary" data-toggle="modal" data-
target="#myModal">
  Launch demo modal
</button>


<!-- Modal -->
<div class="modal fade" id="myModal" tabindex="-1" role="dialog" aria-
labelledby="exampleModalLabel" aria-hidden="true">
  <div class="modal-dialog" role="document">
    <div class="modal-content">
      <div class="modal-header">
        <h5 class="modal-title" id="exampleModalLabel">Modal title</h5>
        <button type="button" class="close" data-dismiss="modal" aria-label="Close">
          <span aria-hidden="true">&times;</span>
        </button>
      </div>
      <div class="modal-body">
        <h2>Modal body heading</h2>
        <p>Modal body text description</p>
      </div>
      <div class="modal-footer">
        <button type="button" class="btn btn-secondary" data-dismiss="modal">Close</
button>
        <button type="button" class="btn btn-primary">Save changes</button>
      </div>
    </div>
  </div>
</div>
```

Forms

```
<form>
  <div class="form-group">
    <label for="exampleInputEmail1">Email address</label>
    <input type="email" class="form-control" id="exampleInputEmail1" aria-
describedby="emailHelp" placeholder="Enter email">
    <small id="emailHelp" class="form-text text-muted">We'll never share your email
with anyone else.</small>
  </div>
  <div class="form-group">
    <label for="exampleInputPassword1">Password</label>
    <input type="password" class="form-control" id="exampleInputPassword1"
placeholder="Password">
  </div>
  <div class="checkbox">
    <label>
      <input type="checkbox"> Check me out
    </label>
  </div>
  <button type="submit" class="btn btn-primary">Submit</button>
</form>
```

Buttons

.btn Needs to be added to all buttons because it adds padding and margin

.btn-* primary, secondary, success, danger, warning, info, light, dark, link

.btn-outline-* primary, secondary, success, danger, warning, info, light, dark, link

.btn-lg Large buttom

.btn-sm Smaller than default button

Example

```
<a class="btn btn-primary" href="#" role="button">Link</a>
<button class="btn btn-secondary" type="submit">Button</button>
```

Carousel

```
<div id="carousel-name" class="carousel slide" data-ride="carousel">
  <ol class="carousel-indicators">
    <li data-target="#carousel-name" data-slide-to="0" class="active"></li>
    <li data-target="#carousel-name" data-slide-to="1"></li>
    <li data-target="#carousel-name" data-slide-to="2"></li>
  </ol>
  <div class="carousel-inner" role="listbox">
    <div class="carousel-item active">
      <img class="d-block img-fluid" src="https://dummyimage.com/900x340/563d7c/
fff&text=+" alt="First slide">
        <div class="carousel-caption d-none d-md-block">
          <h3>Carousel Slider Title</h3>
          <p>Description text to further describe the content of the slide image</p>
          <a href="" class="btn btn-primary">Call to Action</a>
        </div>
    </div>
    <div class="carousel-item">
      <img class="d-block img-fluid" src="https://dummyimage.com/900x340/563d7c/
fff&text=+" alt="Third slide">
        <div class="carousel-caption d-none d-md-block">
          <a href="" class="btn btn-primary">Call to Action</a>
        </div>
    </div>
  </div>
  <a class="carousel-control-prev" href="#carousel-name" role="button" data-
slide="prev">
    <span class="carousel-control-prev-icon" aria-hidden="true"></span>
    <span class="sr-only">Previous</span>
  </a>
  <a class="carousel-control-next" href="#carousel-name" role="button" data-
slide="next">
    <span class="carousel-control-next-icon" aria-hidden="true"></span>
    <span class="sr-only">Next</span>
  </a>
</div>
```

Jumbotron

```
<div class="jumbotron jumbotron-fluid">
  <div class="container">
    <h1 class="display-3">Fluid jumbotron</h1>
    <p class="lead">This is a modified jumbotron that occupies the entire horizontal
space of its parent.</p>
  </div>
</div>
```

Card

```
<div class="card" style="width: 20rem;">
  <img class="card-img-top w-100" src="https://dummyimage.com/600x400/563d7c/fff"
alt="Card image cap" >
  <div class="card-body">
    <h4 class="card-title">Card title</h4>
    <p class="card-text">Some quick example text to build on the card title and make up
the bulk of the card's content.</p>
    <a href="#" class="btn btn-primary">Go somewhere</a>
  </div>
</div>
```

Breadcrumbs

```
<ol class="breadcrumb">
  <li><a href="#">Home</a></li>
  <li><a href="#">Library</a></li>
  <li class="active">Data</li>
</ol>
```

Responsive embed

```
<div class="embed-responsive embed-responsive-16by9">
  <iframe class="embed-responsive-item" src="..."></iframe>
</div>
```

Tabs

```html
<ul class="nav nav-tabs" id="myTab">
  <li class="nav-item">
    <a class="nav-link active" data-toggle="tab" href="#tabOne">Tab 1</a>
  </li>
  <li class="nav-item">
    <a class="nav-link" data-toggle="tab" href="#tabTwo">Tab 2</a>
  </li>
</ul>
<div class="tab-content pt-3" id="myTabContent">
  <div class="tab-pane fade active show" id="tabOne">Tab One Content</div>
  <div class="tab-pane fade" id="tabTwo">Tab Two Content</div>
</div>
```

Alerts

```html
<div class="alert alert-warning alert-dismissible fade show" role="alert">
  <strong>Note</strong> This alert is dismissable.
  <button type="button" class="close" data-dismiss="alert" aria-label="Close">
    <span aria-hidden="true">&times;</span>
  </button>
</div>
```

Collapse

```html
<a class="btn btn-primary mb-3 collapsed" data-toggle="collapse"
href="#collapseContent" role="button" aria-expanded="false" aria-
controls="collapseContent"><span class="if-collapsed"><b>+</b> Show Content</span>
  <span class="if-not-collapsed"><b>-</b> Hide Content</span></a>
<div class="collapse" id="collapseContent">
  <div class="card card-body">Collapse Content</div>
</div>
<style> /* this custom CSS is used to toggle the button text */
[data-toggle="collapse"].collapsed .if-not-collapsed,
[data-toggle="collapse"]:not(.collapsed) .if-collapsed {display: none;}
</style>
```

Tables

```
<table class="table">
  <thead class="thead-dark">
    <tr>
      <th>#</th>
      <th>thead-dark</th>
    </tr>
  </thead>
  <tbody>
    <tr>
      <th scope="row">1</th>
      <td>Nina</td>
    </tr>
  </tbody>
</table>
```

Dropdowns

```
<div class="dropdown">
  <button class="btn btn-secondary dropdown-toggle" type="button" id="dropdown" data-toggle="dropdown" aria-haspopup="true"
aria-expanded="false">Dropdown Actions</button>
<div class="dropdown-menu" aria-labelledby="dropdown">
    <a class="dropdown-item" href="#">Action One</a>
    <a class="dropdown-item" href="#">Action Two</a>
    <a class="dropdown-item" href="#">Action Three</a>
</div>
</div>
```

Learn Bootstrap 4 and Responsive Design Basics.. Fast!

Learn More

BootstrapQuickStart.com

Component CSS Format and Media Queries

```css
/*
 * Component section heading
 *
 * Component description and use
 */

/* base - shared styles */
.component { width: 220px; }

/* Sub-component with component name as a prefix to isolate styles and
break the cascade. */

.component-heading {
  display: block;
  width: 100px;
  font-size: 1rem;
}

/* variant - alert color */
.component-alert {
  color: #ff0000;
}

/* variant - success color */
.component-success {
  color: #00ff00;
}

/* Add media queries below components instead of a separate stylesheet
or section to make updating easier */

@media (min-width: 480px) {
  .component-heading { width:auto; }
}
```

Alphabetical Index of CSS Classes

.active

.accordion

.alert

.alert-(primary, secondary, success, danger, warning, info, light, dark)

.alert-dismissible

.alert-heading

.alert-link

.align-(baseline, top, middle, bottom, text-top, text-bottom)

.align-content-(sm, md, lg, xl)-(around, between, center, end, start, stretch)

.align-items-(sm, md, lg, xl)-(baseline, center, end, start, stretch)

.align-self-(sm, md, lg, xl)-(auto, baseline, center, end, start, stretch)

.arrow

.badge

.badge-(primary, secondary, success, danger, warning, info, light, dark)

.badge-pill

.bg-(primary, secondary, success, danger, warning, info, light, dark, transparent, white)

.blockquote

.blockquote-footer

.border-(light, dark primary, secondary, transparent, white, warning, success, info, danger, 0, top-0, right-0, bottom-0, left-0)

.border-(bottom, left, right, top)

.breadcrumb

.breadcrumb-item

.bs-popover-(auto, bottom, left, right, top)

.bs-tooltip-(auto, bottom, left, right, top)

.btn

.btn-block

.btn-group

.btn-group-(sm, lg)

.btn-group-toggle

.btn-group-vertical

.btn-(sm, lg)

.btn-link

.btn-outline-(primary, secondary, success, danger, warning, info, light, dark)

.btn-(primary, secondary, success, danger, warning, info, light, dark)

.btn-toolbar

.card

.card-body

.card-columns

.card-deck

.card-footer

.card-group

.card-header

.card-header-pills

.card-header-tabs

.card-img

.card-img-bottom

.card-img-overlay

.card-img-top

.card-link

.card-subtitle

.card-text

.card-title

.carousel

Bootstrap 4

.carousel-caption

.carousel-control-(next, prev)

.carousel-control-(next, prev)-icon

.carousel-fade

.carousel-indicators

.carousel-inner

.carousel-item

.carousel-item-(left, right)

.carousel-item-(next, prev)

.clearfix

.close

.col

.col-(sm, md, lg, xl)-(1-12)

.col-auto

.col-form-label

.col-form-label-(sm, lg)

.collapse

.collapsing

.container

.container-fluid

.custom-checkbox

.custom-control

.custom-control-inline

.custom-control-input

.custom-control-label

.custom-file

.custom-file-control

.custom-file-input

.custom-file-label

.custom-radio

.custom-range

.custom-select

.custom-select-(sm, lg)

.custom-switch

.d-(sm, md, lg, xl)-(none, inline, inline-

block, block, table, table-cell, table-row, flex, inline-flex)

.d-print-(block, inline, inline-block, none, flex, inline-flex, table, table-cell, print-table-row)

.disabled

.display-(1, 2, 3, 4)

.dropdown

.dropdown-divider

.dropdown-header

.dropdown-item

.dropdown-item-text

.dropdown-menu

.dropdown-menu-right

.dropdown-menu-(sm, md, lg, xl)-(right, left)

.dropdown-toggle

.dropdown-toggle-split

.dropleft

.dropright

.dropup

.embed-responsive

.embed-responsive-(16by9, 1by1, 21by9, 3by4)

.embed-responsive-item

.fade

.figure

.figure-caption

.figure-img

.fixed-bottom

.fixed-top

.flex-(sm, md, lg, xl)-(row, row-reverse, column)

.flex-(sm, md, lg, xl)-(nowrap, wrap, wrap-reverse)

.flex-column

.flex-column-reverse

.flex-fill

.flex-grow-*

.flex-shrink-*

.float-(sm, md, lg, xl)-(none, left, right)

.focus

.font-italic

.font-weight-(bold, bolder, light, lighter, normal)

.form-check

.form-check-inline

.form-check-input

.form-check-label

.form-control

.form-control-file

.form-control-(sm, lg)

.form-control-plaintext

.form-control-range

.form-group

.form-inline

.form-row

.form-text

.h-(100, 75, 50, 25, auto)

.(h1-h6)

.hide

.img-fluid

.img-thumbnail

.initialism

.input-group

.input-group-append

.input-group-(sm, lg)

.input-group-prepend

.input-group-text

.invalid-feedback

.invalid-tooltip

.invisible

.is-invalid

.is-valid

.jumbotron

.jumbotron-fluid

.justify-content-(sm, md, lg, xl)-(start, end, center, between, around)

.lead

.list-group

.list-group-flush

.list-group-item

.list-group-item-action

.list-group-item-(primary, secondary, success, danger, warning, info, light, dark)

.list-(inline, inline-item, unstyled)

.m(t,b,r,l,x,y)-(sm, md, lg, xl)-(0, 1, 2, 3, 4, 5, n1, n2, n3, n4, n5)

.mark

.media

.media-body

.mh-100

.modal

.modal-backdrop

.modal-body

.modal-content

.modal-dialog

.modal-dialog-centered

.modal-footer

.modal-header

.modal-(sm, lg)

.modal-open

.modal-scrollbar-measure

.modal-title

.nav

Bootstrap 4

.nav-fill

.nav-item

.nav-justified

.nav-link

.nav-pills

.nav-tabs

.navbar

.navbar-brand

.navbar-collapse

.navbar-(dark, light)

.navbar-expand-(sm, md, lg, xl)

.navbar-nav

.navbar-text

.navbar-toggler

.navbar-toggler-icon

.no-gutters

.offset-(sm, md, lg, xl)-(1-12)

.order-(sm, md, lg, xl)-first

.order-(sm, md, lg, xl)-last

.order-(sm, md, lg, xl)-(0-12)

.p(t,b,r,l,x,y)-(sm, md, lg, xl)-(0, 1, 2, 3, 4, 5, n1, n2, n3, n4, n5)

.overflow-(auto, hidden)

.page-item

.page-link

.pagination

.pagination-(sm, lg)

.popover

.popover-body

.popover-header

.position-(absolute, fixed, relative, static, sticky)

.pre-scrollable

.progress

.progress-bar

.progress-bar-animated

.progress-bar-striped

.rounded

.rounded-(top, right, bottom, left, circle, pill, 0)

.rounded-circle

.row

.shadow-(none, sm, lg)

.show

.showing

.small

.spinner-(border, border-sm, grow, grow-sm)

.sr-only

.sr-only-focusable

.tab-content

.tab-pane

.table

.table-active

.table-bordered

.table-borderless

.table-hover

.table-(primary, secondary, success, danger, warning, info, light, dark)

.table-responsive-(sm, md, lg, xl)

.table-sm

.table-striped

.text-(primary, secondary, success, danger, warning, info, light, dark, muted, white, decoration-none, reset)

.text-hide

.text-justify

.text-(sm, md, lg, xl)-(center, left, right)

.text-(lowercase, uppercase, capitalize, black-50, body, monospace, white-50)

.text-(wrap, nowrap)

.text-truncate

.text-warning

.thead-dark

.thead-light

.toast

.toast-(body, header)

.tooltip

.tooltip-inner

.valid-feedback

.valid-tooltip

.vh-100

.vw-100

.visible

.w-(100, 75, 50, 25)

.was-validated

.w-auto

Convert Pixels to REMS

Pixels	REMS	Pixels	REMS
1 px	0.0625	26	1.625
2 px	0.125	27	1.6875
3 px	0.1875	28	1.75
4 px	0.25	29	1.8125
5 px	0.3125	30	1.875
6 px	0.375	31	1.9375
7 px	0.4375	32	2
8 px	0.5	33	2.0625
9 px	0.5625	34	2.125
10 px	0.625	35	2.1875
11 px	0.6875	36	2.25
12 px	0.75	37	2.3125
13 px	0.8125	38	2.375
14 px	0.875	39	2.4375
15 px	0.9375	40	2.5
Default Bootstrap 4 font size 16 px	1	41	2.5625
17 px	1.0625	42	2.625
18 px	1.125	43	2.6875
19 px	1.1875	44	2.75
20 px	1.25	45	2.8125
21 px	1.3125	46	2.875
22 px	1.375	47	2.9375
23 px	1.4375	48	3
24 px	1.5	49	3.0625
25 px	1.5625	50	3.125

Multiples of Common Units of Measure

Multiples of 15		Multiples of 30	
15	405	30	810
30	420	60	840
45	435	90	870
60	450	120	900
75	465	150	930
90	480	180	960
105	495	210	990
120	510	240	1020
135	525	270	1050
150	540	300	1080
165	555	330	1110
180	570	360	1140
195	585	390	1170
210	600	420	1200
225	615	450	1230
240	630	480	1260
255	645	510	1290
270	660	540	1320
285	675	570	1350
300	690	600	1380
315	705	630	1410
330	720	660	1440
345	735	690	1470
360	750	720	1500
375	765	750	1530
390	780	780	1560

Default Text Sizes

Bootstrap's font sizes are calculated off of the body font size by using rem values. If you change the body font size all styles will be increased/decreased automatically. Rem stands for "root em" because it calculates the size based on the size of the root of the document or body tag.

Tag / Class	Default Font size
body	16px; line-height: 1.5; font-family: "Helvetica Neue", Helvetica, Arial, sans-serif;
p, li	1rem / 16px
h1	2.5rem / 40px
h1 small	80% / 32px
h2	2rem / 32px
h2 small	80% / 25.6px
h3	1.75rem / 28px
h3 small	80% / 22.4px
h4	1.5rem / 24px
h4 small	80% / 24px
h5	1.25rem / 20px
h5 small	80% / 16px
h6	1rem / 16px
h6 small	80% / 12.8px
.display-1	6rem / 90px
.display-2	5.5rem / 82.5px
.display-3	4.5rem / 67.5px
.display-4	3.5rem / 52.5px

Flexbox Reference

Flexbox Reference

Below is flexbox example markup. You could apply flexbox CSS properties manually, but things can get cumbersome when you are trying to apply responsive functionality. The benefit of using Bootstrap 4 flexbox utility classes is that you can set flexbox properties and target specific breakpoints.

What is Flexbox?

In Bootstrap 3 and for the majority of websites, the only way to build multi-column layouts was to set column widths and use floats. Then on mobile, you would just remove the float and width property so that it would change to be one column.

Now with flexbox, or flexible box, you will be able to build complex grid layouts with more control and flexibility to adapt the layout as the viewport changes.

If you are familiar with an UL and LI relationship, flexbox is very similar in how it has sub items or flexbox items inside a parent wrapping container. But since flexbox is a display property it can be applied to any parent and child HTML elements and does not have its own HTML element like `<flexbox>`.

```
<div class="flex-container">

  <div class="flex-item-a">flex item with a class .flex-item-a</div>

  <div>flex item</div>

  <div>flex item</div>

</div>
```

The following pages compares vanilla CSS flexbox to Bootstrap 4 flexbox utility classes to help you decide which approach is best for your situation.

Flex Container

Flex layout gives the container the ability to alter its items' width/height (and order) to best fill the available space of the container.

The container has a main axis and cross axis which depends on the flex direction. Each axis has a start and end. For example, if you set the flex direction to column. The main axis is vertical and the cross axis is horizontal. If you set the flex direction to row, the main axis is horizontal and the cross axis is vertical.

flex-direction: row

flex-direction: column

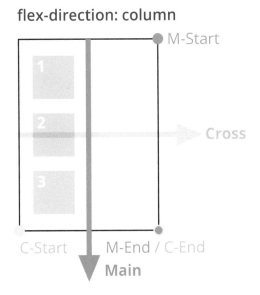

flex-direction: row-reverse

flex-direction: column-reverse

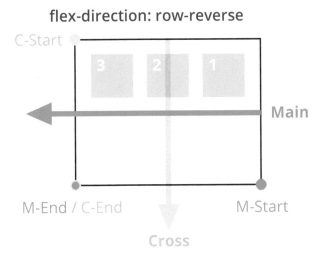

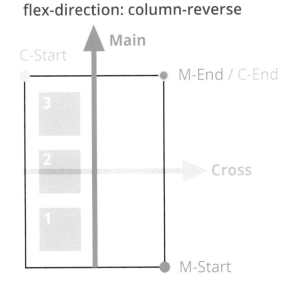

Step 1: Do you want the container to behave like a block or inline element?

CSS	Bootstrap 4

`display:`
 	
Docs: https://developer.mozilla.org/en-US/docs/Web/CSS/display#Values
 	
flex
 	
makes the container act display block
 	
inline-flex
 	
makes the container act display inline
	Use one or a combination of classes below to specify what breakpoints you would like the properties to be applied.
	
	Docs: http://getbootstrap.com/docs/4.0/utilities/flex/#enable-flex-behaviors
	
	`.d-flex`
	
	`.d-inline-flex`
	
	`.d-(sm, md, lg, xl)-(flex, inline-flex)`

FLEXBOX CONTAINER

Step 2: Do you want your main axis to be vertical or horizontal?

CSS	Bootstrap 4

`flex-direction:`
 	
 Docs: https://developer.mozilla.org/en-US/docs/Web/CSS/flex-direction
 	
 row (default)
 	
 left to right
 	
 row-reverse
 	
 right to left
 	
 column
 	
 top to bottom
 	
 column
 	
 reverse = bottom to top
	Use one or a combination of classes below to specify what breakpoints you would like the properties to be applied.
	
	 Docs: http://getbootstrap.com/docs/4.0/utilities/flex/#direction
	
	 `.flex-row`
	
	 `.flex-row-reverse`
	
	 `.flex-column`
	
	 `.flex-column-reverse`
	
	 `.flex-(sm, md, lg, xl)-(row, row-reverse, column, column-reverse)`

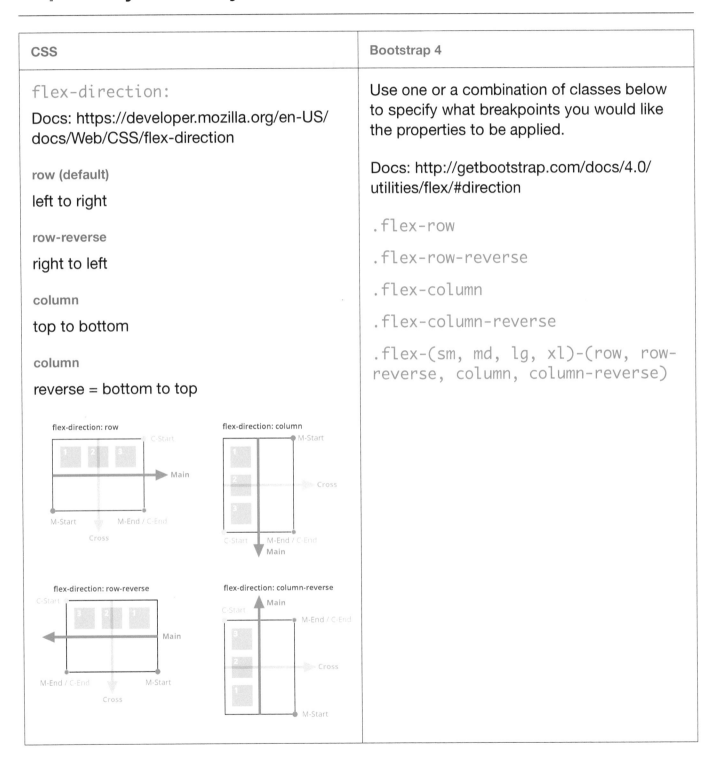

FLEXBOX CONTAINER

Step 3: How do you want the extra space to be distributed along the main axis?

CSS	Bootstrap 4

`justify-content:`
 	
Docs: https://developer.mozilla.org/en-US/docs/Web/CSS/justify-content
 	
flex-start (default)
 	
items anchored to the start
 	
flex-end
 	
items anchored to the start
 	
center
 	
items centered
 	
space-between
 	
items evenly distributed in the line. First item in on the start and last item is at the end
 	
space-around
 	
start and end items are not to the edge but have 1 unit of space on each side
 	
space-evenly
 	
similar to space-around, except all space is the same
	Use one or a combination of classes below to specify what breakpoints you would like the properties to be applied.
	
	Docs: http://getbootstrap.com/docs/4.0/utilities/flex/#justify-content
	
	`.justify-content-start`
	
	`.justify-content-end`
	
	`.justify-content-center`
	
	`.justify-content-between`
	
	`.justify-content-around`
	
	`.justify-content-(sm, md, lg, xl)-(start, end, center, between, around)`

FLEXBOX CONTAINER

Step 4: How do you want the extra space of LINES of items to be distributed along the cross axis?

CSS	Bootstrap 4

`align-content:`
 	
Docs: https://developer.mozilla.org/en-US/docs/Web/CSS/align-content
 	
flex-start
 	
items anchored to the start
 	
flex-end
 	
items anchored to the end
 	
center
 	
items centered
 	
space-between
 	
first line at the start of the container and the last one is at the end
 	
space-around
 	
lines are evenly distributed with equal space around each line
 	
stretch (default)
 	
lines stretch to take up the space that is left
	Use one or a combination of classes below to specify what breakpoints you would like the properties to be applied.
	
	Docs: http://getbootstrap.com/docs/4.0/utilities/flex/#align-content
	
	`.align-content-start`
	
	`.align-content-end`
	
	`.align-content-center`
	
	`.align-content-around`
	
	`.align-content-stretch`
	
	`.align-content-(sm, md, lg, xl)-(start, end, center, around, stretch)`

FLEXBOX CONTAINER

Step 5: How do you want the extra space between items to be distributed along the cross axis?

CSS	Bootstrap 4

`align-items:`
 	
Docs: https://developer.mozilla.org/en-US/docs/Web/CSS/align-items
 	
flex-start
cross axis align items to start
 	
flex-end
cross axis align items to end
 	
center
cross axis align items center
 	
baseline
align baselines
 	
stretch (default)
stretch to fill the container
	Use one or a combination of classes below to specify what breakpoints you would like the properties to be applied.
	
	Docs: http://getbootstrap.com/docs/4.0/utilities/flex/#align-items
	
	`.align-items-start`
	
	`.align-items-end`
	
	`.align-items-center`
	
	`.align-items-baseline`
	
	`.align-items-stretch`
	
	`.align-items-(sm, md, lg, xl)-(start, end, center, baseline, stretch)`

FLEXBOX CONTAINER

Step 6: Want the items to wrap if they don't fit on one line?

CSS	Bootstrap 4

`flex-wrap:`
 	
Docs: https://developer.mozilla.org/en-US/docs/Web/CSS/flex-wrap
 	
nowrap (default)
 	
all items will try to stay on one line
 	
wrap
 	
if items don't fit they will wrap and create a new line below
 	
wrap-reverse
 	
if items don't fit they will wrap and create a new line above
	Use one or a combination of classes below to specify what breakpoints you would like the properties to be applied.
	
	Docs: http://getbootstrap.com/docs/4.0/utilities/flex/#wrap
	
	`.flex-nowrap`
	
	`.flex-wrap`
	
	`.flex-wrap-reverse`
	
	`.flex-(sm, md, lg, xl)-(nowrap, wrap, wrap-reverse)`

Shorthand property

This is a shorthand property that sets the `flex-direction` and `flex-wrap` properties. I suggest avoid using this until you learn the core properties because it could make things more confusing.

CSS	Bootstrap 4
`flex-flow:` Docs: https://developer.mozilla.org/en-US/docs/Web/CSS/flex-flow **< flex-direction > < flex-wrap >** example: `flex-flow: column-reverse wrap-reverse;` or just `flex-flow: wrap-reverse;`	Since Bootstrap uses classes there is no shorthand property available.

Flex Item

Do you want to override the parent settings and give a specific item their own unique settings?
You will first need to write a custom class and add it to the item you would like to modify.

- Flexbox items follow the orders given by their container.
- By default, flex items all want to appear on the same line
- Individual flexbox items can be targeted with a unique class and property to override the orders given by their container. The example below uses the class .flex-item-a to make adjustments to only flex-item-a

Example:

HTML

```
<div class="flex-container">
  <div class="flex-item-a">.flex-item-a</div>
  <div class="flex-item-b">.flex-item-b</div>
  <div class="flex-item-c">.flex-item-c</div>
</div>
```

CSS

```
.flex-item-a {
  order: 3;
  font-weight: bold;
}
```

Result

.flex-item-b	.flex-item-c	**.flex-item-a**

FLEXBOX ITEM

Step 1: Do you want to change the order of this item relative to the other items?

CSS	Bootstrap 4

`order:`
 	
Docs: https://developer.mozilla.org/en-US/docs/Web/CSS/order
 	
[number]
 	
default is 0
	Use one or a combination of classes below to specify what breakpoints you would like the properties to be applied.
	
	Docs: http://getbootstrap.com/docs/4.0/utilities/flex/#order
	
	`.order-(1-12)`
	
	`.order-sm-(1-12)`
	
	`.order-md-(1-12)`
	
	`.order-lg-(1-12)`
	
	`.order-xl-(1-12)`

FLEXBOX ITEM

Step 2: Do you want to have this item take up more space than the other items?

CSS	Bootstrap 4
`flex-grow:` Docs: https://developer.mozilla.org/en-US/docs/Web/CSS/flex-grow [number] default is 0	No classes available

FLEXBOX ITEM

Step 3: Do you want this item to take less space than the other items?

CSS	Bootstrap 4
flex-shrink: Docs: https://developer.mozilla.org/en-US/docs/Web/CSS/flex-shrink [number] default is 0	No classes available

FLEXBOX ITEM

Step 4: Do you want to set the default size of this item before the other item sizes are set?

CSS	Bootstrap 4
flex-basis: Docs: https://developer.mozilla.org/en-US/docs/Web/CSS/flex-basis [length] A number followed by px, em, rem, or %. Check the docs for additional keywords auto (default) look at my width or height property	No classes available

FLEXBOX ITEM

Step 5: Do you want to override the align-items value for this item?

CSS	Bootstrap 4

`align-self:`
 	
Docs: https://developer.mozilla.org/en-US/docs/Web/CSS/align-self
 	
auto
 	
inherits the parent container's align-items property
 	
flex-start
 	
cross-start margin is on the cross start line
 	
flex-end
 	
cross-end margin is on the cross end line
 	
center
 	
centers are aligned
 	
baseline
 	
baselines are aligned
 	
stretch (default)
 	
fill the container
	Use one or a combination of classes below to specify what breakpoints you would like the properties to be applied.
	
	Docs: http://getbootstrap.com/docs/4.0/utilities/flex/#align-self
	
	`.align-self-start`
	
	`.align-self-end`
	
	`.align-self-center`
	
	`.align-self-baseline`
	
	`.align-self-stretch`
	
	`.align-self-sm-(start, end, center, baseline, stretch)`
	
	`.align-self-md-(start, end, center, baseline, stretch)`
	
	`.align-self-lg-(start, end, center, baseline, stretch)`
	
	`.align-self-xl-(start, end, center, baseline, stretch)`

Shorthand property

This is the shorthand for flex-grow, flex-shrink and flex-basis combined.

CSS	Bootstrap 4
`flex:` Docs: https://developer.mozilla.org/en-US/docs/Web/CSS/flex **example:** Three values: flex-grow | flex-shrink | flex-basis `flex: 2 2 10%;`	Since Bootstrap uses classes there is no shorthand property available

Colors Reference

Colors Reference

How to use RGBA in your CSS

```
.rgba-color {color: rgba(2, 117, 216, 0.5);}
```

RGBA is a lot like light shining through a stained glass window. The more light that shines through the window, the brighter the color. The less light shining through the window, the color becomes darker. RGBA stands for red, green, blue, and alpha. Each color has a maximum value of 255. If all RGB values are the same you will have a gray value. The maximum value for Alpha is 1, which means 100%. A lower alpha value will allow background colors ot show through.

Code example: https://codepen.io/JacobLett/pen/eRPeyj

Key

A: Link hover

B: Input focus border color

C: Primary

D: Primary alert background

E: Secondary

F: Secondary alert background

G: Success

H: Success alert background

I: Danger

J: Danger alert background

K: Warning

L: Warning alert background

M: Info

N: Info alert background

O: Light

P: Light alert background

Q: Dark

R: Dark alert background

BootstrapCreative

Primary

	HEX	RGB
	# 007bff	0.123.255
A	# 0069d9	0.105.217
B	# 80bdff	128.189.255

Grays

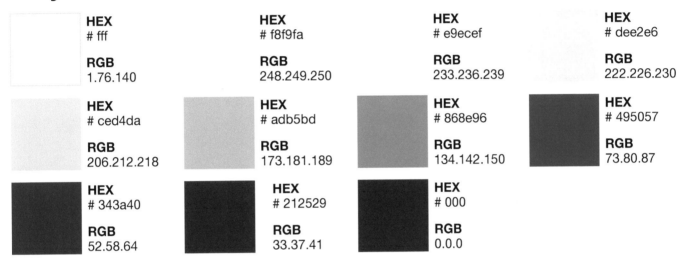

HEX	RGB
# fff	1.76.140
# f8f9fa	248.249.250
# e9ecef	233.236.239
# dee2e6	222.226.230
# ced4da	206.212.218
# adb5bd	173.181.189
# 868e96	134.142.150
# 495057	73.80.87
# 343a40	52.58.64
# 212529	33.37.41
# 000	0.0.0

Contextual

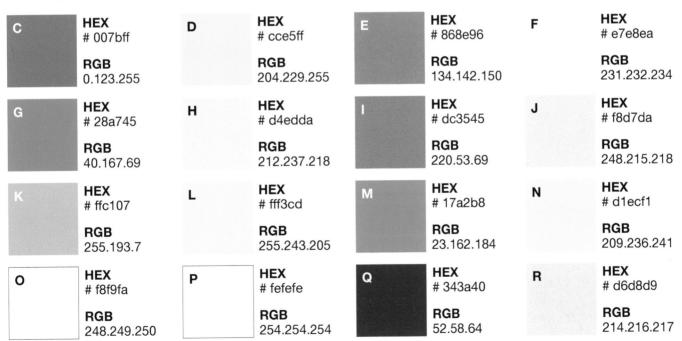

	HEX	RGB
C	# 007bff	0.123.255
D	# cce5ff	204.229.255
E	# 868e96	134.142.150
F	# e7e8ea	231.232.234
G	# 28a745	40.167.69
H	# d4edda	212.237.218
I	# dc3545	220.53.69
J	# f8d7da	248.215.218
K	# ffc107	255.193.7
L	# fff3cd	255.243.205
M	# 17a2b8	23.162.184
N	# d1ecf1	209.236.241
O	# f8f9fa	248.249.250
P	# fefefe	254.254.254
Q	# 343a40	52.58.64
R	# d6d8d9	214.216.217

CSS Variables

```
<!-- note that the :root is required -->
:root {
  --blue: #007bff;
  --indigo: #6610f2;
  --purple: #6f42c1;
  --pink: #e83e8c;
  --red: #dc3545;
  --orange: #fd7e14;
  --yellow: #ffc107;
  --green: #28a745;
  --teal: #20c997;
  --cyan: #17a2b8;
  --white: #fff;
  --gray: #6c757d;
  --gray-dark: #343a40;
  --primary: #007bff;
  --secondary: #6c757d;
  --success: #28a745;
  --info: #17a2b8;
  --warning: #ffc107;
  --danger: #dc3545;
  --light: #f8f9fa;
  --dark: #343a40;
  --breakpoint-xs: 0;
  --breakpoint-sm: 576px;
  --breakpoint-md: 768px;
  --breakpoint-lg: 992px;
  --breakpoint-xl: 1200px;
  --font-family-sans-serif: -apple-system,
BlinkMacSystemFont, "Segoe UI", Roboto,
"Helvetica Neue", Arial, sans-serif,
"Apple Color Emoji", "Segoe UI Emoji",
"Segoe UI Symbol";
  --font-family-monospace: SFMono-Regular,
Menlo, Monaco, Consolas, "Liberation
Mono", "Courier New", monospace;
}
```

How to use these

CSS variables are supported in most modern browsers except for IE11 and below. For current browser support please reference https://caniuse.com/#feat=css-variables

Below is an example on how you can use these variables for your custom components.

Example

```
.class-name {
  color: var(--blue);
}
```

 BootstrapCreative

Bootstrap 3

Bootstrap 3.4.0

CSS

```
<link rel="stylesheet" href="https://stackpath.bootstrapcdn.com/bootstrap/3.4.0/css/
bootstrap.min.css" integrity="sha384-PmY9l28YgO4JwMKbTvgaS7XNZJ30MK9FAZjjzXtlqyZCqBY6X
6bXIkM++IkyinN+" crossorigin="anonymous">
```

JS

```
<script src="https://ajax.googleapis.com/ajax/libs/jquery/1.12.4/jquery.min.js"></
script>
<script src="https://stackpath.bootstrapcdn.com/bootstrap/3.4.0/js/bootstrap.min.js"
integrity="sha384-vhJnz1OVIdLktyixHY4Uk3OHEwdQqPppqYR8+5mjsauETgLOcEynD9oPHhhz18Nw"
crossorigin="anonymous"></script>
```

CSS

- Typography
- Code
- Tables
- Forms
- Buttons
- Images
- Helper classes
- Responsive utilities

JavaScript

- Transitions
- Modal
- Dropdown
- Scrollspy
- Tab
- Tooltip
- Popover
- Alert
- Button
- Collapse
- Carousel
- Affix

Components

- Glyphicons
- Dropdowns
- Button groups
- Button dropdowns
- Input groups
- Navs
- Navbar
- Breadcrumbs
- Pagination
- Labels
- Badges
- Jumbotron
- Page header
- Thumbnails
- Alerts
- Progress bars
- Media object
- List group
- Panels
- Responsive embed
- Wells

BootstrapCreative

Grid

Basic grid - full width is 12 columns wide

```
<!-- change .container to .container-fluid
to be full width -->
<div class="container">
 <!-- Columns are always 50% wide, on
mobile and desktop -->
 <div class="row">
   <div class="col-xs-6">.col-xs-6</div>
   <div class="col-xs-6">.col-xs-6</div>
 </div>
 <!-- nested columns example -->
 <div class="row">
   <div class="col-xs-6">.col-xs-6</div>
   <div class="col-xs-6">.col-xs-6
   <div class="row">
     <div class="col-md-6">100% mobile
50% everywhere else</div>
     <div class="col-md-6">100% mobile
50% everywhere else</div>
   </div>
  </div>
 </div>
</div>
```

Media queries

```
/* Extra small devices (phones, less than
768px) No media query since this is the
default in Bootstrap */
/* small (tablets, 768px and up) */
@media (min-width: @screen-sm-min) { ... }
/* medium (desktops, 992px and up) */
@media (min-width: @screen-md-min) { ... }
/* large (large desktops, 1200px and up)
*/
@media (min-width: @screen-lg-min) { ... }
```

Text & Images

`.text-left` Left aligned text

`.text-center` Center aligned text

`.text-right` Right aligned text

`.text-justify` Justified text

`.text-nowrap` No wrap text

`.text-lowercause` Lowercase text

`.text-uppercase` Uppercase text

`.text-capitalize` Capitalized text

`.lead` Good for first paragraph of article

`.list-unstyled` Removes default list margin/padding

`.list-inline` Makes list items inline

`.dl-horizontal` Makes list items two columns

`.img-responsive` Make an image responsive

`.img-rounded` Adds rounded corners to image

`.img-circle` Crops image to be circle

`.img-thumbnail` Adds rounded corner and border to an image

`.pull-left` Floats item left

`.pull-right` Floats item right

`.center-block` Set an elemennt to block with auto left and right margin

`.clearfix` Clear floats by adding this class to the parent container

Blockquote

```
<blockquote><p>Lorem ipsum dolor</p>
<footer>Someone famous in <cite
title="Source Title">Source Title</
cite></footer></blockquote>
```

Headings

```
<h1>h1. Bootstrap heading
<small>Secondary text</small></h1>
<p class="h1">Paragraph that looks like
heading</p>
```

Navbar

```
<!-- Fixed top navbar with brand as logo image tags -->
<nav class="navbar navbar-default navbar-fixed-top">
  <div class="container-fluid">
    <!-- Brand and toggle get grouped for better mobile display -->
    <div class="navbar-header">
      <button type="button" class="navbar-toggle collapsed" data-toggle="collapse"
data-target="#bs-example-navbar-collapse-1" aria-expanded="false">
        <span class="sr-only">Toggle navigation</span>
        <span class="icon-bar"></span>
        <span class="icon-bar"></span>
        <span class="icon-bar"></span>
      </button>
      <a class="navbar-brand" href="#"><img alt="Brand" src="..."></a>
    </div>
    <!-- Collect the nav links, forms, and other content for toggling -->
    <div class="collapse navbar-collapse" id="bs-example-navbar-collapse-1">
      <ul class="nav navbar-nav">
        <li class="active"><a href="#">Link <span class="sr-only">(current)</span></a></li>
        <li><a href="#">Link</a></li>
        <li class="dropdown">
          <a href="#" class="dropdown-toggle" data-toggle="dropdown" role="button"
aria-haspopup="true" aria-expanded="false">Dropdown <span class="caret"></span></a>
          <ul class="dropdown-menu">
            <li><a href="#">Action</a></li>
            <li role="separator" class="divider"></li>
            <li><a href="#">Separated link</a></li>
          </ul>
        </li>
      </ul>
    </div><!-- /.navbar-collapse -->
  </div><!-- /.container-fluid -->
</nav>
```

Forms

```
<form>
  <div class="form-group">
    <label for="exampleInputEmail1">Email address</label>
    <input type="email" class="form-control" id="exampleInputEmail1"
placeholder="Email">
  </div>
  <div class="form-group">
    <label for="exampleInputPassword1">Password</label>
    <input type="password" class="form-control" id="exampleInputPassword1"
placeholder="Password">
  </div>
  <div class="form-group">
    <label for="exampleInputFile">File input</label>
    <input type="file" id="exampleInputFile">
    <p class="help-block">Example block-level help text here.</p>
  </div>
  <div class="checkbox">
    <label><input type="checkbox"> Check me out</label>
  </div>
  <button type="submit" class="btn btn-default">Submit</button>
</form>
```

Buttons

.btn Needs to be added to all buttons because it adds padding and margin

.btn-default The default button style

.btn-primary The button that has the primary action in a group

.btn-success Could be used on the last submit button in a form

.btn-info Informational button

.btn-link Removes background color and add text color

.btn-(lg,sm, xs) Large buttom, smaller than default button, even smaller

.btn-block Button that spans full width of parent

Example

```
<a class="btn btn-default" href="#" role="button">Link</a>
```

Carousel

```
<div id="carousel-example-generic" class="carousel slide" data-ride="carousel">
  <!-- Indicators -->
  <ol class="carousel-indicators">
    <li data-target="#carousel-example-generic" data-slide-to="0" class="active"></li>
    <li data-target="#carousel-example-generic" data-slide-to="1"></li>
  </ol>
  <!-- Wrapper for slides -->
  <div class="carousel-inner" role="listbox">
    <div class="item active">
      <img src="..." alt="...">
      <div class="carousel-caption">
        ...
      </div>
    </div>
    <div class="item">
      <img src="..." alt="...">
      <div class="carousel-caption">
        ...
      </div>
    </div>
    ...
  </div>
  <!-- Controls -->
  <a class="left carousel-control" href="#carousel-example-generic" role="button" data-slide="prev">
    <span class="glyphicon glyphicon-chevron-left" aria-hidden="true"></span>
    <span class="sr-only">Previous</span>
  </a>
  <a class="right carousel-control" href="#carousel-example-generic" role="button" data-slide="next">
    <span class="glyphicon glyphicon-chevron-right" aria-hidden="true"></span>
    <span class="sr-only">Next</span>
  </a>
</div>
```

Jumbotron

```
<div class="jumbotron">
  <h1>Hello, world!</h1>
  <p>...</p>
  <p><a class="btn btn-primary btn-lg" href="#" role="button">Learn more</a></p>
</div>
```

To make the jumbotron full width, and without rounded corners, place it outside all .containers and instead add a .container within.

```
<div class="jumbotron">
  <div class="container">...</div>
</div>
```

Page header

```
<div class="page-header">
  <h1>Example page header <small>Subtext for header</small></h1>
</div>
```

Breadcrumbs

```
<ol class="breadcrumb">
  <li><a href="#">Home</a></li>
  <li><a href="#">Library</a></li>
  <li class="active">Data</li>
</ol>
```

Responsive embed

```
<!-- 16:9 aspect ratio - change aspect ratio by replacing 16by9 with 4by3 -->
<div class="embed-responsive embed-responsive-16by9">
  <iframe class="embed-responsive-item" src="..."></iframe>
</div>
```

Tables

```
<!-- Responsive table with all of the options applied  -->
<div class="table-responsive">
  <table class="table table-condensed table-hover table-bordered table-striped">
 <tr class="active">...</tr>
 <tr>
   <td class="info">...</td>
 </tr>
   </table>
</div>
```

Alphabetical Index of CSS Classes

.active

.affix

.alert

.alert-danger

.alert-dismissible

.alert-info

.alert-link

.alert-success

.alert-warning

.arrow

.badge

.bg-danger

.bg-info

.bg-primary

.bg-success

.bg-warning

.bottom

.breadcrumb

.btn

.btn-block

.btn-danger

.btn-default

.btn-group

.btn-group-justified

.btn-group-vertical

.btn-info

.btn-link

.btn-primary

.btn-sm

.btn-success

.btn-toolbar

.btn-warning

.btn-xs

.caption

.caret

.carousel

.carousel-caption

.carousel-control

.carousel-indicators

.carousel-inner

.center-block

.checkbox

.checkbox-inline

.close

.col-lg-* /*(1-12)*/

.col-lg-offset-* /*(0-12)*/

.col-lg-pull-* /*(0-12)*/

.col-lg-push-* /*(0-12)*/

.col-md-* /*(1-12)*/

.col-md-offset-* /*(0-12)*/

.col-md-pull-* /*(0-12)*/

.col-md-push-* /*(0-12)*/

.col-sm-* /*(1-12)*/

.col-sm-offset-* /*(0-12)*/

.col-sm-pull-* /*(0-12)*/

.col-sm-push-* /*(0-12)*/

.col-xs-* /*(1-12)*/

.col-xs-offset-* /*(0-12)*/

.col-xs-pull-* /*(0-12)*/

.col-xs-push-* /*(0-12)*/

.collapse

.collapsing

.container

.container-fluid

.control-label

.divider

Bootstrap 3

.dropdown

.dropdown-backdrop

.dropdown-header

.dropdown-menu

.dropdown-menu-left

.dropdown-menu-right

.dropdown-toggle

.embed-responsive

.embed-responsive-16by9

.embed-responsive-4by3

.fade

.form-control

.form-control-feedback

.form-control-static

.form-group

.glyphicon

.glyphicon-chevron-left

.glyphicon-chevron-right

.h1

.h2

.h3

.h4

.h5

.h6

.has-feedback

.help-block

.hidden

.hidden-lg

.hidden-md

.hidden-print

.hidden-sm

.hidden-xs

.hide

.icon-bar

.icon-next

.icon-prev

.img-circle

.img-rounded

.img-thumbnail

.in

.initialism

.input-group

.input-group-addon

.input-group-btn

.input-lg

.input-sm

.invisible

.item

.jumbotron

.label

.label-danger

.label-default

.label-info

.label-primary

.label-success

.label-warning

.lead

.left

.list-group

.list-group-item

.list-group-item-danger

.list-group-item-heading

.list-group-item-info

.list-group-item-success

.list-group-item-text

.list-group-item-warning

.list-inline

.list-unstyled

.mark

.media

.media-body

.media-heading

.media-list

.media-object

.modal

.modal-backdrop

.modal-body

.modal-content

.modal-dialog

.modal-footer

.modal-header

.modal-lg

.modal-open

.modal-scrollbar-measure

.modal-sm

.modal-title

.nav

.nav-divider

.nav-justified

.nav-tabs

.nav-tabs-justified

.navbar

.navbar-brand

.navbar-btn

.navbar-collapse

.navbar-default

.navbar-fixed-bottom

.navbar-fixed-top

.navbar-form

.navbar-header

.navbar-inverse

.navbar-left

.navbar-link

.navbar-nav

.navbar-right

.navbar-static-top

.navbar-text

.navbar-toggle

.next

.page-header

.pager

.pagination

.panel

.panel-body

.panel-danger

.panel-default

.panel-footer

.panel-group

.panel-heading

.panel-info

.panel-primary

.panel-success

.panel-title

.panel-warning

.popover

.popover-content

.popover-title

.pre-scrollable

.prev

.progress

.progress-bar

.progress-bar-danger

.progress-bar-info

.progress-bar-striped

.progress-bar-success

.progress-bar-warning

.pull-left

.pull-right

.right

.row

Bootstrap 3

.row-no-gutters
.show
.small
.sr-only
.tab-pane
.table
.table-bordered
.table-responsive
.text-capitalize
.text-center
.text-danger
.text-hide
.text-info
.text-justify
.text-left
.text-lowercase
.text-muted
.text-nowrap
.text-primary
.text-right
.text-success
.text-uppercase
.text-warning
.thumbnail
.tooltip
.tooltip-arrow
.tooltip-inner
.top
.visible-lg
.visible-lg-block
.visible-lg-inline
.visible-lg-inline-block
.visible-md
.visible-md-block
.visible-md-inline

.visible-md-inline-block
.visible-print
.visible-print-block
.visible-print-inline
.visible-print-inline-block
.visible-sm
.visible-sm-block
.visible-sm-inline
.visible-sm-inline-block
.visible-xs
.visible-xs-block
.visible-xs-inline
.visible-xs-inline-block
.well
.well-lg
.well-sm

CSS Reference

CSS Reference

HTML defines the page content and CSS styles it. CSS stands for Cascading Style Sheets and applys the visual style to the page content. CSS uses the "box model" to describe HTML elements.

The CSS box model is a container that wraps around each elements and contains layers. It consists of the content, padding, border, and margin.

Content - The content of the box, where text and images appear

Padding - Clears an area around the content. The padding is transparent

Border - A border that goes around the padding and content

Margin - Clears an area outside the border. The margin is transparent

Color Key:

Content   Padding   Border   Margin

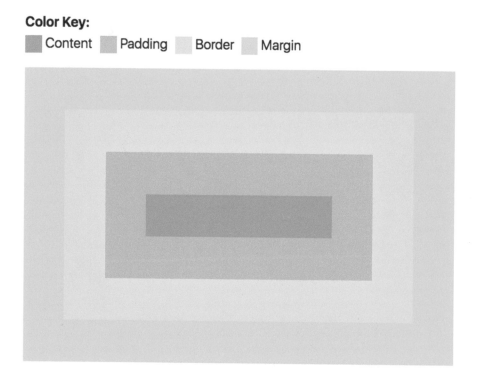

CSS Selectors

CSS Vendor Prefixes

.class

#id

*

element

element,element

element element

element>element

element+element

element1~element2

[attribute]

[attribute=value]

[attribute~=value]

[attribute|=value]

[attribute^=value]

[attribute$=value]

[attribute*=value]

Combinators

(space) descendant selector

> child selector

+ adjacent sibling selector

~ general sibling selector

Pseudo Elements

::after

::before

::first-letter

::first-line

::selection

Pseudo Classes

:active

:checked

:disabled

:empty

:enabled

:first-child

:first-of-type

:focus

:hover

:in-range

:invalid

:lang(language)

:last-child

:last-of-type

:link

:not(selector)

:nth-child(n)

:nth-last-child(n)

:nth-last-of-type(n)

:nth-of-type(n)

:only-of-type

:only-child

:optional

:out-of-range

:read-only

:read-write

:required

:root

:target

:valid

:visited

-ms-
Microsoft

mso-
Microsoft Office

-moz-
Mozilla Foundation (Gecko-based browsers)

-o-, -xv-
Opera Software

-atsc-
Advanced Television Standards Committee

-wap-
The WAP Forum

-webkit-
Safari, Chrome (and other WebKit-based browsers)

-khtml-
Konqueror browser

-apple-
Webkit supports properties using the
-apple-
prefixes as well

prince-
YesLogic

-ah-
Antenna House

-hp-
Hewlett Packard

-ro-
Real Objects

-rim-
Research In Motion

-tc-
Tall Components

CSS Units

cm
centimeters

mm
millimeters

in
inches (1in = 96px = 2.54cm)

px
pixels (1px = 1/96th of 1in)

pt
points (1pt = 1/72 of 1in)

pc
picas (1pc = 12 pt)

em
Relative to the font-size of the element

ex
Relative to the x-height of the current font (rarely used)

ch
Relative to width of the "0" (zero)

rem
Relative to font-size of the root element

vw
Relative to 1% of the width of the viewport*

vh
Relative to 1% of the height of the viewport*

vmin
Relative to 1% of viewport's* smaller dimension

vmax
Relative to 1% of viewport's* larger dimension

%
Relative to the parent element

CSS Functions

attr()
Returns the value of an attribute of the selected element

calc()
Allows you to perform calculations to determine CSS property values

cubic-bezier()
Defines a Cubic Bezier curve

hsl()
Defines colors using the Hue-Saturation-Lightness model (HSL)

hsla()
Defines colors using the Hue-Saturation-Lightness-Alpha model (HSLA)

linear-gradient()
Sets a linear gradient as the background image. Define at least two colors (top to bottom)

radial-gradient()
Sets a radial gradient as the background image. Define at least two colors (center to edges)

repeating-linear-gradient()
Repeats a linear gradient

repeating-radial-gradient()
Repeats a radial gradient

rgb()
Defines colors using the Red-Green-Blue model (RGB)

rgba()
Defines colors using the Red-Green-Blue-Alpha model (RGBA)

var()
Inserts the value of a custom property

Default CSS Property Values

animation : none;

animation-delay : 0;

animation-direction : normal;

animation-duration : 0;

animation-fill-mode : none;

animation-iteration-count : 1;

animation-name : none;

animation-play-state : running;

animation-timing-function : ease;

backface-visibility : visible;

background : 0;

background-attachment : scroll;

background-clip : border-box;

background-color : transparent;

background-image : none;

background-origin : padding-box;

background-position : 0 0;

background-position-x : 0;

background-position-y : 0;

background-repeat : repeat;

background-size : auto auto;

border : 0;

border-style : none;

border-width : medium;

border-color : inherit;

border-bottom : 0;

border-bottom-color : inherit;

border-bottom-left-radius : 0;

border-bottom-right-radius : 0;

border-bottom-style : none;

border-bottom-width : medium;

border-collapse : separate;

border-image : none;

border-left : 0;

border-left-color : inherit;

border-left-style : none;

border-left-width : medium;

border-radius : 0;

border-right : 0;

border-right-color : inherit;

border-right-style : none;

border-right-width : medium;

border-spacing : 0;

border-top : 0;

border-top-color : inherit;

border-top-left-radius : 0;

border-top-right-radius : 0;

border-top-style : none;

border-top-width : medium;

bottom : auto;

box-shadow : none;

box-sizing : content-box;

caption-side : top;

clear : none;

CSS Reference

clip : auto;

color : inherit;

columns : auto;

column-count : auto;

column-fill : balance;

column-gap : normal;

column-rule : medium none currentColor;

column-rule-color : currentColor;

column-rule-style : none;

column-rule-width : none;

column-span : 1;

column-width : auto;

content : normal;

counter-increment : none;

counter-reset : none;

cursor : auto;

direction : ltr;

display : inline;

empty-cells : show;

float : none;

font : normal;

font-family : inherit;

font-size : medium;

font-style : normal;

font-variant : normal;

font-weight : normal;

height : auto;

hyphens : none;

left : auto;

letter-spacing : normal;

line-height : normal;

list-style : none;

list-style-image : none;

list-style-position : outside;

list-style-type : disc;

margin : 0;

margin-bottom : 0;

margin-left : 0;

margin-right : 0;

margin-top : 0;

max-height : none;

max-width : none;

min-height : 0;

min-width : 0;

opacity : 1;

orphans : 0;

outline : 0;

outline-color : invert;

outline-style : none;

outline-width : medium;

overflow : visible;

overflow-x : visible;

overflow-y : visible;

padding : 0;

padding-bottom : 0;

padding-left : 0;

padding-right : 0;

padding-top : 0;

page-break-after : auto;

page-break-before : auto;

BootstrapCreative

page-break-inside : auto;

perspective : none;

perspective-origin : 50% 50%;

position : static;

/* May need to alter quotes for different locales (e.g fr) */

quotes : '\201C' '\201D' '\2018' '\2019';

right : auto;

tab-size : 8;

table-layout : auto;

text-align : inherit;

text-align-last : auto;

text-decoration : none;

text-decoration-color : inherit;

text-decoration-line : none;

text-decoration-style : solid;

text-indent : 0;

text-shadow : none;

text-transform : none;

top : auto;

transform : none;

transform-style : flat;

transition : none;

transition-delay : 0s;

transition-duration : 0s;

transition-property : none;

transition-timing-function : ease;

unicode-bidi : normal;

vertical-align : baseline;

visibility : visible;

white-space : normal;

widows : 0;

width : auto;

word-spacing : normal;

z-index : auto;

CSS Component Structure

One important thing to understand is Bootstrap is focused around components and utility classes. When writing your custom styles it is recommended to keep your styles organized by component instead of pages.

If you are creating a new component that is not part of Bootstrap, you can write it in the format shown in the example to the right. Start with your base styles that all variations have in common so you are not redundant with styles.

Next, write your sub component styles and variation styles. Any media queries styles should be added underneath each component and not in a separate stylesheet. This will greatly improve future maintenance because you will know what styles are impacted when a component changes.

```css
/*
 * Component section heading
 *
 * Component description and use
 */

/* base - shared styles */
.component { width: 220px; }

/* Sub-component */
.component-heading {
  display: block;
  width: 100px;
  font-size: 1rem;
}

/* variant - alert color */
.component-alert {
  color: #ff0000;
}

/* variant - success color */
.component-success {
  color: #00ff00;
}


@media (min-width: 480px) {
  .component-heading { width:auto; }
}
```

Responsive Images

How to create Responsive Images

The two biggest limitations of smartphones are the slow internet connection speeds and small screens. Responsive images help to improve the user experience by loading the optimal image size based on their screen size. HTML provides two ways of doing this, Using the `<picture>` element or adding srcset to an existing img tag.

Picture Element

The picture element gives you a lot of control on how your image looks on different breakpoints and retina displays. As you resize your window the browser will load the necessary image.
It takes more work up-front to build the images but the control is worth it in prominent locations like carousels.

- CodePen of various image proportions.
- If you need to support IE11 and below use this polyfill.

When to Use

- When you want to change how an image looks on different breakpoints (size, cropping, etc.)
- Carousels and Image cards

```
<picture>
  <source srcset="https://dummyimage.com/2000x400/000/fff"
media="(min-width: 1400px)">
  <source srcset="https://dummyimage.com/1400x400/000/fff"
media="(min-width: 768px)">
  <source srcset="https://dummyimage.com/800x400/000/fff"
media="(min-width: 576px)">
  <img srcset="https://dummyimage.com/600x400/000/fff" alt=""
class="d-block img-fluid">
</picture>
<!-- If a picture looks blurry on a retina device you can add a high res img like this -->
<source srcset="img/blog-post-1000x600-2.jpg, blog-post-
1000x600-2@2x.jpg 2x" media="(min-width: 768px)">
```

Image srcset

Image srcset is an attribute added to an image tag and provides various images for the browser to use depending on the viewport width. It is best used when you need little control on how it is cropped and sized. But you want to speed up page load on mobile and get rid of image pixilation on retina displays. If you need to support IE11 and below use this polyfill.

One challenge with this solution is that the image is loaded on page load and does not change when the browser is resized due to image caching. To work around this, I found using the Chrome extension Cache Killer helps when testing sites.

When to Use

- Blog post images
- Any image you want to look the same (same proportions and image) but just want to increase resolution.

```
<img src="https://dummyimage.com/400x200/000/fff"
srcset="https://dummyimage.com/800x400/000/fff 1000w, https://
dummyimage.com/1600x600/000/fff 2000w, https://dummyimage.
com/1600x600/000/fff 2x" alt="">
```

Image Format Comparison

BMP

The BMP file format (Windows bitmap) are usually uncompressed, and therefore large and lossless.

- **Characteristics:** Raster, lossless
- **Downsides:** Larger file size
- **When to Use:** Windows applications

JPG/JPEG

JPEG (Joint Photographic Experts Group) is a lossy compression method and the most common image format on the web.

- **Characteristics:** Raster, lossy
- **Downsides:** Does not have transparency
- **When to Use:** Photographs with a lot of gradients and colors.

TIFF

The TIFF (Tagged Image File Format) format is can be saved without compression and CMYK color profiles. So it is best used for high quality images in print design.

- **Characteristics:** Raster, lossless
- **Downsides:** Large file size
- **When to Use:** Best used for print and should use JPG as an alternative.

GIF

GIF (Graphics Interchange Format) is most suitable for storing graphics with few colors, such as simple diagrams, shapes, logos, and cartoon style images. It is also widely used to provide image animation effects.

- **Characteristics:** Raster, lossless
- **Downsides:** Saving indexes colors and downgrades quality
- **When to Use:** Animations mostly because PNG8 is a better alternative.

PNG8

The PNG (Portable Network Graphics) file format was created as a free, open-source alternative to GIF.

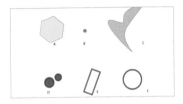

- **Characteristics:** Raster, transparency, lossless
- **Downsides:** Only supports 256 colors.
- **When to Use:** Logos, icons, line illustrations. A GIF substitute.

PNG32

The PNG (Portable Network Graphics) file format was created as an open-source alternative to GIF.

- **Characteristics:** Raster, transparency, lossless
- **Downsides:** File sizes can get large
- **When to Use:** When you want a photograph jpeg with transparency, images with gradients

SVG

SVG (Scalable Vector Graphics) is an open standard for a versatile, scriptable and all-purpose vector format for the web.

- **Characteristics:** Vector, transparency
- **Downsides:** Harder to setup and often requires javascript to load
- **When to Use:** Icons, logos, text you want to be high quality on retina displays

WEBP

Created by Google, WebP is a modern image format that provides superior lossless and lossy compression for images on the web. 25-34% smaller than comparable JPEG and PNG images.

- **Characteristics:** Raster, transparency
- **Downsides:** Currently (2019) not supported on IE, FIrefox, or Safari.
- **When to Use:** For everything as long as your browser supports it. Or you can provide image fallbacks.

Lossy vs lossless?

When saving images, some formats use compression-algorithms that either delete information (lossy) or keep all image information (lossless). Lossless images are larger in size but make it easier to open and re-edit images if necessary.

Photo Editing Software

Desktop

- Adobe Photoshop
- Gimp
- Affinity Photo

Online

- Photopea
- Canva
- Pixlr

Additional Reference

CSS Rule Set

A rule set is a single section of CSS including the selector, the curly braces, and the different lines with properties and values. The code in the example below comprises one rule set.

Selector

Declaration Block

Curly Braces

Property

Value

```css
.btn {
    display: inline-block;
    padding: .5rem 1rem;
    border-radius: .25rem;
    border: 1px solid;
}
```

The Parts of a URL

The URL, or uniform resource locator, above corresponds to the folder structure shown to the right. You have the option to not use the www subdomain by redirecting any traffic you receive to just your domain. The query string starts with a ? and all additional parameters start with a &.

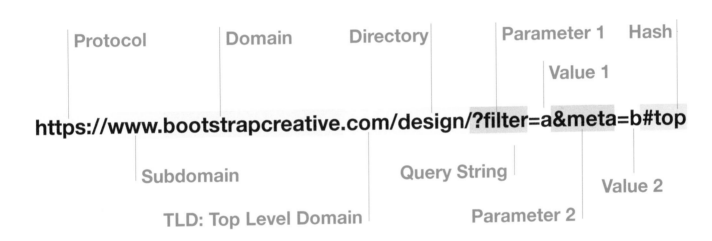

jQuery and the DOM

jQuery is a DOM (Document Object Model) manipulation library. The DOM is a tree-structure representation of all the elements of a Web page. jQuery simplifies the syntax for finding, selecting, and manipulating these DOM elements.

Javascript comments

Calls the Bootstrap 4 Tooltip Function and Runs It

Document Ready Function

jQuery DOM Selector

camelCase Variable Names and Prefix jQuery Variables with $

```javascript
$(function() {
    // enable toggles everywhere
    $('[data-toggle="tooltip"]').tooltip();

    var variableName = "global variable";
    var $bodyID = $("body").attr("id");
    console.log("Body ID #" + $bodyID);
    // Body ID #home


}); // document ready - end
```

Console Log Function Writes a Message in Chrome Dev Tools. Use for Testing.

HTML Element Parts

Short for HyperText Markup Language, the authoring language used to create documents on the World Wide Web. HTML defines the structure and layout of a web document by using a variety of tags and attributes.

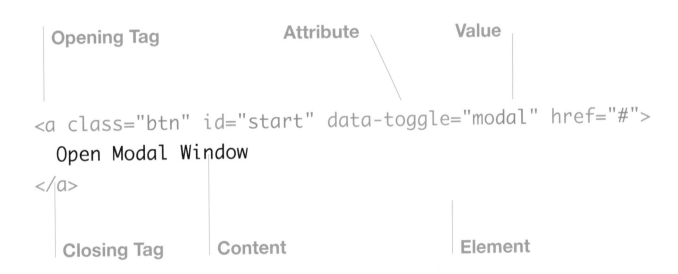

HTML, CSS, JavaScript Naming

A general rule for all naming is to write all characters lowercase and use hyphens instead of spaces between words. If you use spaces your URL will have %20 in it which is hard to read in print.

HTML

- Lowercase
- Avoid inline styles
- For quick scanning, write classes first
- Always include closing HTML tags
- Only use an ID if absolutely necessary

Example

```
<div class="btn btn-default"
id="bt-action"></div>
```

CSS

- Lowercase with hyphens between words
- Short as possible without obscuring readability. Avoid names like .s etc.
- Prefix classes based on the closest parent or base class.

Example

```
.btn {}
.btn-primary {}
#btn-action {}
```

JavaScript

- camelCase
- Short as possible without obscuring readability. Avoid variables like `var a` etc.
- jQuery objects should start with $ as prefix. This will help you remember what variables are objects.

Example

```
var $ctaBtn = $("#btn-action");
$ctaBtn.fadeIn("slow");
```

Things I Wish I Knew Sooner

Know and embrace common aspect ratios (21:9, 16:9, 4:3, 3:2).

When creating layouts you will often place videos and images at pre-determined proportions. Your design will be more cohesive if you use those proportions for other elements like carousel images and product images.

A great design doesn't guarantee great results.

Design and test for the majority of users and focus on making it a great experience there first. Use tools like Google Analytics and Hotjar to monitor how people use your site and look for ways to make things easier to use. If you have never used these tools, you will be surprised to find your beautiful design doesn't actually achieve the goals your first set out to solve.

Your client or boss could love your design at launch and three months later ask you why they are not getting leads or not ranking #1 for a certain keyword phrase.

GitHub projects can have multiple versions of files stored inside one folder on your machine called branches.

If you switch branches with GitHub desktop the files are changed automatically to the new branch. This was a mental shift for me because I was so used to having different versions of projects in different folders on my computer. I was also afraid of losing or overriding something.

Designing and building responsive websites require 3x the time & effort of a static desktop site.

Make sure you factor time in for quality assurance testing after you complete the initial build. Responsive design requires buy-in from designers, developers, writers, and executives.

Feelings of failure are normal.

No matter how much I learn I will always have times when I experience feelings of inferiority. Sometimes I get assigned a new project and I cannot figure it out. Everything I try doesn't work and I have exhausted every Google search I could think of. The longer the problem goes without being solved the worse I feel. Then I start asking myself questions like, "How can you be a developer if you can't solve this?" or "Your boss is going to think you are a fraud and will fire you for not knowing how to solve this." Sound familiar?

What has helped me is allowing more time necessary to learn. Often I would force myself to solve something by the end of the day or before lunch. Sometimes it just takes more time to solve the problem we are facing. Taking a break and do something not computer related helps to clear our mind. So many times I have struggled with some code for an entire day and being so stubborn to stop until it was fixed. Then when I finally did take a break, I would come back and find the smallest thing causing the problem. Like a period instead of a comma. : /

CSS Code Best Practices

· Try and list properties in this order: 1. Positioning, 2. Box model (display, float, width, etc), 3. Typography (font, line-height), 4. Visuals (background, border, opacity), 5. Misc (CSS3 properties)

· Any rule set with multiple declarations should be split to separate lines because syntax errors on Line numbers would be hard to find.

· Use soft-tabs set to two spaces, set encoding to UTF-8

· When using multiple CSS files, break them down by component instead of page.

· Keep media queries as close to their relevant rule sets whenever possible. Don't bundle them all in a separate stylesheet or at the end of the document.

· Do not use @import because it slows down page load.

· Place closing braces of declaration blocks on a new line.

· End all declarations with a semi-colon to prevent errors.

· Lowercase all hex values. For example, #fff instead of #FFF.

· Avoid specifying units for zero values. For example, margin: 0; instead of margin: 0px;.

Inspired by Code Guide by Mark Otto: http://codeguide.co/

Design Inspiration

- **Bootstrap Expo**
  https://expo.getbootstrap.com/
- **Built With Bootstrap**
  http://builtwithbootstrap.com/
- **Wrap Bootstrap**
  https://wrapbootstrap.com/
- **Official Bootstrap Themes**
  https://themes.getbootstrap.com/
- **AWWWARDS**
  https://www.awwwards.com/websites/
  responsive-design/
- **Media Queries**
  https://mediaqueri.es/
- **Pattern Tap**
  http://zurb.com/patterntap
- **CodePen Pattern Library**
  http://codepen.io/patterns/
- **Building Blocks**
  http://foundation.zurb.com/building-
  blocks/

HTML Reference

- **Mozilla HTML Reference**
  https://developer.mozilla.org/en-US/docs/
  Web/HTML
- **HTMLReference.io**
  https://htmlreference.io/

CSS Reference

- **Mozilla CSS Reference**
  https://developer.mozilla.org/en-US/docs/
  Web/CSS/Reference
- **CSS-Tricks Almanac**
  https://css-tricks.com/almanac/
- **Can I Use?**
  https://caniuse.com/
- **CSSreference.io**
  https://cssreference.io/

JavaScript Reference

- **Mozilla JavaScript Reference**
  https://developer.mozilla.org/en-US/docs/
  Web/JavaScript/Reference
- **jQuery Documentation**
  https://api.jquery.com/

Bootstrap Reference

- **Bootstrap 4 Classes Reference**
  https://bootstrapcreative.com/resources/
  bootstrap-4-css-classes-index/
- **Bootstrap 3 Classes Reference**
  https://bootstrapcreative.com/resources/
  bootstrap-3-css-classes-index/
- **Official Bootstrap Documentation**
  http://getbootstrap.com/
- **Bootsnip - Bootstrap Code Snippets**
  https://bootsnipp.com/

Want to Save Time Using Bootstrap 4?

Get project starter templates, reference guides, and more!

Bootstrap 4 Toolkit

Learn More

bootstrapcreative.com/b4toolkit

Bootstrap Snippets and UI Examples Library

A collection of code snippets to help you quickly customize components.
Includes the necessary HTML, CSS, and JS you need to implement in your project.

https://bootstrapcreative.com/pattern/

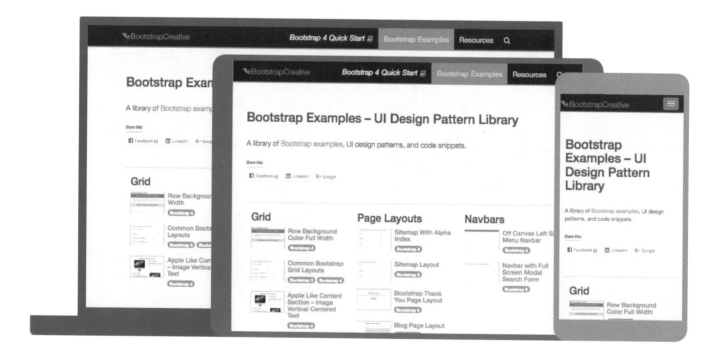

Notes

Notes

Thank you!

I hope you have found this Bootstrap reference guide helpful and informative.

Let's make a responsive web together!

Sign up to recieve free book updates and future training.

https://bootstrapcreative.com/signup

Find an error? Or have a suggestion on how this book could be improved?

Please contact support@bootstrapcreative.com

CPSIA information can be obtained
at www.ICGtesting.com
Printed in the USA
LVHW070013290620
659242LV00018B/1877

* 9 7 8 1 7 3 2 2 0 5 8 3 3 *